Blank

French Adjectives and Adverbs with Prepositions

Copyright © 2011 by Pascal d'Herve

Cover and Book design by Pascal d'Herve

All rights reserved.

No part of this book may be reproduced in any form or by any electronic or mechanical means including information storage and retrieval systems, without permission in writing from the author. The only exception is by a reviewer, who may quote short excerpts in a review.

ISBN #: 978-1-4476-6711-7

Preface

Following the book " French verbs with Prepositions", here is "French Adjectives and adverbs with prepositions", it is difficult to speak fluently a new language without knowing the difference between our own language and the one we want to learn.

The way to build sentences are important to know, as we cannot all the times translate from English to French word to word.
For example, let's take two adjectives, difficile (difficult) and essentiel (essential) and these two sentences:

- It is difficult to understand whe he is saying
- I am ready to go

In these two exemples, we have the word "to" following the adjective, let's see the translation in French:

- C'est difficile de comprendre ce qu'il dit
- Je suis prêt à partir

In the first sentence, we have the preposition "de" and in the second one "à" to translate "to" in English. Even if we use to say that "from, of" are translated as "de", it is not allways like that.

Adjectives or adverbs with preposition are also linked to idioms, expressions you cannot guess and need to know to express correctly.

In this book we are not going to see all the adjectives and adverbs followed by a preposition, some are easy to translate, but the most useful expressions, this way you will be able to learn them all and to improve your vocabulary.

Most of the adjectives have a feminine form, some are regular, you need to add a final "e", some are irregular, you will find them too (of course the adjective ended in "e" have the same feminine form)

Reading this book on a device will make your life easy, with the "search" feature you will go straight to the verb you are looking for. However, you can start learning them by heart as they are all very useful in a day-to-day conversation.

If you need to refresh your French with vocabulary or grammar easy to undersand, visit http://www.frenchspanishonline.com.

Mini Dictionary of French Adjectives and Adverbs

Letter A

Absent: à, de, pour, pendant

> Meaning: absent, away, missing
> Feminine form: absente
> Plural: absents, absentes

Il était absent à la reunion (he was not AT the meeting): he did not attend the meeting.
Je serai absent de mon travail (absent FROM): I will be off work.
Je (girl) serai absente de mon travail (absent FROM): I will be off work.
Elle est absente de Londres (absent FROM): she is away from London.
Nous sommes absents pour deux demaines: we will be absent for 2 weeks.

So for this adjective, you now understand that we can translate "at" as "à" and "from" as "de".
Absent à and **absent de** are interchangeable, but absent de is most used.

Adhérent: à

> Meaning: adherent, member
> Feminine form: adhérente
> Plural: adhérents, adhérentes

Les personnes non adhérentes au club: non members of the club.
les pneus sont adhérents à la route (adhere to): the tyres are with good road-hoalding.

Adjacent: à

> Meaning: adjacent, near
> Feminine form: adjacente
> Plural: adjacents, adjacentes

Cette pièce est adjacente à la cuisine: this room is adjacent to the kitchen.

Admissible: à

> Meaning: admissible, eligible
> Feminine form: admissible
> Plural: admissibles

Il est admissible à l'oral: he is eligible to sit the oral part of the exam.

Adroit: à, de

> Meaning: skilful, clever
> Feminine form: adroite
> Plural: adroits, adroites

Il est adroit au travail: he is skilful at work.
Elle est adroite de ses mains: she is clever with her hand.

Affamé: de

> Meaning: starving, greedy
> Feminine form: affamée
> Plural: affamés, affamées

Il est affamé de gloire: he is greedy for fame.

Âgé: de

> Meaning: old
> Feminine form: âgée
> Plural: âgés, âgées.

Il est âgé de 28 ans: he is 28 years old.

Agile: à, de

> Meaning: agile, nimble
> Feminine form: agile
> Plural: agiles

Ils ont des mains agiles au travail: they are nimble with their fingers at work.
Ils sont agiles de leurs mains: they are nimble with their fingers.

Agréable: à, avec, de, en

> Meaning: pleasant, nice
> Feminine form: agréable
> Plural: agréables

C'est agréable à voir, à faire...: it is nice to see, to do...
Il est toujours agréable avec ses parents: he is always pleasant with his parents.
C'est agréable de ne rien faire: it is nice to do nothing.
Ell est agréable de sa personne: she is pleasant-looking.
Ils sont agréables en société: they are pleasant in society.

C'est agréable à voir means that it is worthy to see something.
C'est agréable de voir means that it is good to be able to see.
C'est agréable de voir son enfant grandir (when there is something after the verb, we use "de").

Allergique: à

> Meaning: allergic
> Feminine form: allergique
> Plural: allergiques

Il est allergique aux champignons, au gluten... : he is allergic to mushrooms, to gluten...

Amoureux: de

> Meaning: in love
> Feminine form: amoureuse
> Plural: amoureux, amoureuse

Il est amoureux de sa voiture: he has a passion for cars.
Il est amoureux de cette fille: he is in love with this girl.

Amusant: à, de

> Meaning: funny
> Feminine form: amusante
> Plural: amusants, amusantes

C'est amusant à voir: it is funny to see.
C'est un livre amusant à lire: it is a book funny to read.
Il est amusant de constater combien les enfants apprennent vite: it is amusing to observe how fast children can learn.

We use "à" when there is nothing after the following verb: c'est amusant à voir (nothing).
We use "de" for general things and also when the sentence is longer: c'est amusant de faire du sport.

Antérieur: à

> Meaning: prior, before
> Feminine form: antérieure
> Plural: antérieurs, antérieures

C'était antérieur à la crise: it was prior to the crisis.
C'était antérieur de 2 semaines: is was before 2 weeks.

We say "à" for things and events, and "de" for periods of time.

Applicable: à

> Meaning: applicable
> Feminine form: applicable
> Plural: applicables

Ce règlement est applicable à tous: this rule is applicable to all.
Règlement applicable à l'assemblée: rule applicable to the assembly.

Appréciable: de

> With no preposition: arrêter quelqu'un or quelque chose
> La police a arrêté le voleur: police arrested the thief.
> On ne peut pas arrêter le progrès: nothing can't stop the progress.

C'est appréciable de ne rien faire: it is nice to do nothing.
Un nombre appréciable de personnes: a good many people.

Approprié: à

> With no preposition: arrêter quelqu'un or quelque chose
> La police a arrêté le voleur: police arrested the thief.
> On ne peut pas arrêter le progrès: nothing can't stop the progress.

Je ne crois pas que cela soit approprié à la situation: I don't believe it is appropiate to the current situation.
C'est un discours approprié aux circonstances: it is a speech suited to the circumstances.

Apte: à

> Meaning: capable, fit, qualified for
> Feminine form: apte
> Plural: aptes

Il est apte au travail: he capable of working.
Il est apte à faire ce travail: he is qualified for this job.
Je ne suis pas apte à juger: I am not able to judge.

Attentif: à

> Meaning: attentive, careful
> Feminine form: attentive
> Plural: attentifs, attentives

Il est attentif à tout ce qui se passe: he pays attention to everything that is going on.
Ell est attentive à son travail: she is careful in her work.
Il est attentif à sa santé: he is mindful of his health.
Elle est attentive aux besoins de sa mère: she is attentive to her mother's needs.

Avide: de

> Meaning: greedy, avid
> Feminine form: avide
> Plural: avides

Il est avide de pouvoir: he is greedy for power.
Les enfants sont avides de nouveautés: the children are eager for novelties.
Il est avide de savoir: he is thirsty to learn..

Letter B

Beau: à

> Meaning: pretty, nice, good-looking
> Feminine form: belle
> Plural: beaux, belles

L'accident n'était pas beau à voir: the accident was not a pretty sight.
La pomme est belle à croquer: The apple looks good enough to eat.

Beaucoup: à, de

> Meaning: a lot of, many, much

Il reste beaucoup à faire: there is a lot to do.
Il y avait beaucoup de monde: there was a lot of people.
Il reste beaucoup de pain? Is there a lot of bread left?

Bienvenu: à, chez, parmi

> Meaning: welcome
> Feminine form: bienvenue
> Plural: bienvenus, bienvenues

Vous êtes bienvenu à la maison: you are welcome home.
Bienvenu chez vous: welcome home.
Bienvenu parmi nous: welcome (among us)

Bon: à, contre, de, en, pour

> Meaning: good
> Feminine form: bonne
> Plural: bons, bonnes

Tu es bon à rien: you are good for nothing.
Le journal est bon à jeter: the newspaper can go straight in the bin.
C'est bon contre ton mal de tête: it is goog for your headache.
C'est bon de te voir: it is good to see you.
Il est très bon en français: he is very good at French.
C'est bon pour la santé: it is good for health.
Il est bon pour une belle amende: he is in for a pretty fine.
J'ai tout effacé par erreur, je suis bon pour ton recommencer: I have erased everything by mistake, I will have to do it all again.

Letter C

Capable: de

> With no preposition: choisir quelqu'un or quelque chose
> Elle a choisi un bon travail: she chose a good job.
> Je choisis Pierre: I choose Pierre.

Je suis capable de le faire. I can do it.
T'es même pas capable de le faire: do it, if you dare!
Il est capable de tout quand il est en colère: he will stop at nothing when he is angry.
Il est bien capable de l'avoir perdu: he is quite likely to have lost it.

Capital: de

> Meaning: essential, important
> Feminine form: capitale
> Plural: capitaux, capitales

Il est capital de terminer à l'heure: it is essential that we finish on time.

Certain: de

> Meaning: sure
> Feminine form: certaine
> Plural: certains, certaines

Tu es certain de le faire? are you sure you will do it?
Je suis certaine de sa sincérité: I am convinced of his sincerity.

Complice: de

> Meaning: accomplice
> Feminine form: complice
> Plural: complices

Il est complice de meurtre: he is accomplice to murder.

Conscient: de

> Meaning: conscious, lucid
> Feminine form: consciente
> Plural: conscients, conscientes

Il n'est pas conscient du danger: he is not aware of the danger.

Content: de

> Meaning: glad, happy
> Feminine form: contente
> Plural: contents, contentes

Je suis content de l'apprendre: I am happy to hear that.
Et tu es content de toi? and you are pleased with yourself?

Contraire: à

> Meaning: opposite, contrary, against
> Feminine form: contraire
> Plural: contraires

C'est contraire au réglement: it goes against the rules.

Contrairement: à

> Meaning: contrary to

Contrairement à ses habitudes: contrary to his habit.
Contrairement à toi, je n'irai pas: unlike you, I won't go.

Correct: avec, en

> Meaning: correct
> Feminine form: correcte
> Plural: corrects, correctes

Il n'a pas été correct avec toi: he has not been correct with you.
Il est correct en affaires: He is correct in business matters.

Coupable: de

> Meaning: guilty
> Feminine form: coupable
> Plural: coupables

Il est coupable de vol: he is guilty of theft.

Curieux: de

> Meaning: curious
> Feminine form: curieuse
> Plural: curieux, curieuses

Il est curieux de tout: he is curious about everything.
Je suis curieux d'apprendre: I am interested in learning.

Letter D

Davantage: de

> Meaning: more
> Feminine form: davantage

Je voudrais davantage de pain: I would like more bread.
Elle a eu davantage de chance que les autres: she was luckier than the others.

Dépendant: à, de

> Meaning: dependent, addicted
> Feminine form: dépendante
> Plural: dépendants, dépendantes

Il est dépendant à la drogue: he is addicted to drugs.
C'est dépendant du temps: it depends on the weather. (ça dépend du temps is most used)
Il est dépendant de sa femme: he is dependent on his wife.

Désireux: de

> Meaning: dependent, addicted
> Feminine form: dépendante
> Plural: dépendants, dépendantes

Je suis désireux de la connaître: I am anxious to make her acquaintance.

Difficile: à, sur

> Meaning: difficult
> Feminine form: difficile
> Plural: difficiles

C'est dificile à faire: it is difficult to do.
C'est difficile de faire cela: It is difficult to do that.
Il est très difficile à satisfaire: he is very hard to please.
Elle est difficile sur le choix des invités: she is particular about the guests.
Il est difficile sur la nourriture: he is fussy about food.

We use **difficile à** for short sentences with nothing after the following verb.
We use **difficile de** for longer sentences with something after.

Digne: de

> Meaning: worthy
> Feminine form: digne
> Plural: dignes

Vous n'êtes pas digne de reprensenter notre société: you are not worthy to represent our company.
Il n'est pas digne de foi: he is not trustworthy.
tu es le digne fils de ton père: you are fit to be your father's son.

Distant: de

> Meaning: far-off, distant
> Feminine form: distante
> Plural: distants; distantes

La boulangerie est distante de 2 km: the bakery is 2 km away..

Drôle: de

> Meaning: funny, odd
> Feminine form: drôle
> Plural: drôles

C'est une drôle d'idée: it is a funny idea.
Il y a une drôle d'odeur: there is a strange smell.

Dupe: de

> Meaning: fool
> Feminine form: dupe
> Plural: dupes

Je ne suis pas dupe de vous: I am not fooled by you.

Dur: à, avec, de, en

> Meaning: hard, harsh
> Feminine form: dure
> Plural: durs, dures

C'est un dur à cuire: he is a hard nut to crack.
C'est dur de faire cela: it is hard to do that.
Tu es trop dur avec lui: you are too harsh with him.
Il est dur en affaires: he is a tough businessman.

Dur à is for short sentences with a verb, **dur de** is for longer sentences.

Letter E

Égal: à, en, entre

> Meaning: equal
> Feminine form: égale
> Plural. égaux, égales

5 est égal à 2 + 3: 5 is equal to 2 plus 3.
Les deux sont égaux en hauteur: they both have the same height.
Elles sont égales entre elles: they are equal.

Enclin: à

> Meaning: prone to
> Feminine form: encline
> Plural: enclins, enclines

Il est enclin à voler: he is prone to robbery.
Il est enclin à aider les autres: he is inclined to help others

Épais: de

> Meaning: thick
> Feminine form: épaisse
> Plural: épais, épaisses

C'est épais de 5 cm: it is 5cm thick.
La planche est épaisse de 5 cm: the board is 5 cm thick.

Essentiel: à

> Meaning: essential
> Feminine form: essentielle
> Plural: essentiels, essentielles

C'est essentiel à la comprehension du texte: it is essential to understand the text.
L'eau est essentielle à la vie: water is essential to life.
C'est essentiel à la compréhension du texte: it is essential for a good understanding of the text.
C'est essentiel pour comprendre le texte: it is essential for a good understanding of the text.

Exact: à

> Meaning: exact, accurate
> Feminine form: exacte
> Plural: exacts, exactes

Il est toujours exact à ses rendez-vous: he always arrives punctually for his appointments.

Excessif: en, de

> Meaning: excessive
> Feminine form: excessive
> Plural: excessifs, excessives

Il est excessif en tout: he is a man of extremes.
C'est excessif de dire qu'il est bête: it is going to far to say he is stupid.

Exempt: de

> Meaning: exempt from, free from
> Feminine form: exempte
> Plural: exempts, exemptes

Le colis est exempt de taxes: the parcel is tax-free.
L'envoi est exempt de port: shipping is carriage free.

Letter F

Facile: à, de

> Meaning: easy
> Feminine form: facile
> Plural: faciles

C'est facile à faire: it is easy to do.
C'est très facile d'emploi: it is easy to use.
Ce n'est pas facile d'expliquer la situation: it is not easy to explain the situation.
C'est très facile d'accès: it is easy to reach.

Facile à is for short sentences with nothing after the following verb (facile à + verb), **facile de** is for longer sentences.

Faible: avec, de, en

> Meaning: weak
> Feminine form: faible
> Plural: faibles

Il est faible de caractère: he has a weak character.
Il est trop faible avec ses enfants: he is too soft with his children.
Il est faible en anglais: he is poor at English.

Fatigant: à, avec, de, pour

> Meaning: tiring, boring
> Feminine form: fatigante
> Plural: fatigants, fatigantes

C'est fatigant à faire: it is tiring to do.
Tu es fatigant avec tes histoires: you are annoying with your stories.
C'est fatigant de devoir crier: it is tiresome to have to shout.
C'est fatigant pour la vue: it is a strain on the eyes.

Fatigant à is for short sentences with nothing after the following verb and **fatigant de** is generally speaking about something or when the sentence is longer: c'est fatigant de devoir crier ton nom.

Fidèle: à, de

> Meaning: faithful
> Feminine form: fidèle
> Plural: fidèles

Je reste fidèle à ma parole: I remain faithful to my word.
Il est fidèle à la tradition: he followes a tradition.
Ce qu'il dit est fidèle à la réalité: what he is saying is a true picture of the situation.
Je suis fidèle à votre émission: I am a regular viewer of your programme.
(however with the noun, we say: je suis un fidèle DE votre émission).

Fort: à, de, en, sur

> Meaning: strong, good
> Feminine form: forte
> Plural: forts, fortes

Elle est forte à la course: she is good at running.
Une armée forte de 5000 hommes: an army 5000 strong.
Elle est un peu forte de la taille: she has rather wide hips.
Cette boisson est forte en café: this drink has a high content of coffee.
Il est fort en français: he is good at French.
Il est fort sur ce sujet: he is good at this subject.

Fou: à, de

> Meaning: mad, crazy
> Feminine form: folle
> Plural: fous, folles

Il est fou à lier (to tie up): he is raving mad.
Elle est folle de joie: she is out of her mind with joy.
Elle est folle de lui: she is mad about him.

Friand: de

> Meaning: fond
> Feminine form: friande
> Plural: friands, friandes

Elle est friande de chocolat: she is fond of chocolate.

Letter G

Généreux: de

> Meaning: generous
> Feminine form: généreuse
> Plural: généreux, généreuses

Il est généreux de son temps: he is generous with his time.
Il se montre généreux envers ses amis: he is generous with his friends.
Il se montre généreux avec ses amis: he is generous with his friends.

Letter H

Habile: à, de

> Meaning: skilful
> Feminine form: habile
> Plural: habiles

Il est habile au tennis: he is skilful at playing tennis.
Elle est habile de ses mains: she is clever with her hands..

Heureux: avec, dans, de, en

> Meaning: happy
> Feminine form: heureuse
> Plural: heureux, heureuses

Je suis heureux avec vous: I am happy with you.
Je suis heureux dans mes choix: I am happy in my choices.
Je suis heureux de l'apprendre: I am very glad to hear that.
Nous sommes heureux de vous annoncer: we are happy to announce.
Je ne suis pas heureux en amour: I am not lucky in love.
Heureux au jeu, malheureux en amour: lucky at cards, unlucky in love.
Ils sont heureux en ménage: they have a happy married life..

Heureux de + verb

Honteux: à, de

> Meaning: shameful
> Feminine form: honteuse
> Plural: honteux, honteuses

Mais il n'y a rien de honteux à cela: but there is nothing to be ashamed of.
Tu devrais être honteux de ta conduite: you should be ashamed of your behaviour.

Honteux à and **être honteux de**

Horrible: avec

> Meaning: horrible
> Feminine form: horrible
> Plural: horribles

Tu a été horrible avec moi: you were horrible to me.

Letter I

Impardonnable: de

> Meaning: unforgivable
> Feminine form: impardonnable
> Plural: impardonnables

Tu es vraiment impardonnable d'avoir fait ça: you cannot be forgiven for doing that.

Impatient: de

> Meaning: impatient
> Feminine form: impatiente
> Plural: impatients, impatientes

Je suis impatient de le revoir: I can't wait to see him again.

Important: à, de

> Meaning: important
> Feminine form: importante
> Plural: importants, importantes

C'est important à savoir: it is an important thing to know.
Il est important de terminer: it is important to finish.

Incapable: de

> Meaning: incapable, incompetent
> Feminine form: incapable
> Plural: incapables

Je suis incable de terminer: I am not able to finish.
Elle est incapable de mentir: she can't lie.

Indifférent: à, de

> Meaning: indifférent
> Feminine form: indifférente
> Plural: indifférents, indifférentes

Je suis indifférent à tes mensonges: I am indifferent at your lies.
Elle est indifférente à la politique: she is indifferent towards politics.
Il m'est indifférent d'y aller maintenat ou plus tard: it does not matter to me whether I go now or later.

Indifférent à is followed with a noun and **indifférent de** with a verb.

Injuste: avec, envers

> Meaning: unfair
> Feminine form: injuste
> Plural: injustes

Tu es injuste avec lui: you are unfair to him.
Tu es injuste envers lui: you are unfair to him.

Envers are synonymous means towards.

Inquiet: au sujet de, de, pour

> Meaning: worried
> Feminine form: inquiète
> Plural: inquiets, inquiètes

Je suis inquiet au sujet de l'entreprise: I am worried about the company.
Je suis inquiet pour l'entreprise: I am worried about the company.
Elle est inquiète de son absence: She's worried about his absence.

Au sujet de, de and pour and nearly interchangeable

Intéressant: à, pour

> Meaning: interesting
> Feminine form: intéressante
> Plural: intéressants, intéressantes

C'est très intéressant à lire: it is very interesting to read.
C'est une personne intéressante à connaître: he is someone worth knowing.
Il est intéressant de remarquer que...: it is interesting to notice that...
Ce n'est pas intéressant pour nous, c'est trop cher: it si not worth our while, it is too expensive.

Inutile: à, de

> Meaning: useless
> Feminine form: inutile
> Plural; inutiles

Le nouvel ordinateur est inutile à Paul: the new computer is useless to Paul.
Inutile d'insister! it is pointless insisting.
Inutile de vous dire que je lui ai dit ce que je pense: needless to say that I told him what I really think.

Inutile à for things and **inutile de** with a verb.

Letter J

Jaloux: de

> Meaning: jealous
> Feminine form: jalouse
> Plural: jaloux, jalouses

Il est jaloux de sa réussite: he is jealous of his success.

Juste: à, envers, de

> Meaning: fair, correct
> Feminine form: juste
> Plural: justes

Il est arrivé juste à temps: he arrived just in time.
Il est juste envers tout le monde: he is fair to everybody.
C'est juste de dire la vérité: it is fair to tell the truth.

Juste de + verb

Letter L

Large: de

> Meaning: wide
> Feminine form: large
> Plural: larges

Ce camion est large de 3 mètres! this trick is 8 meters wide.
Le bateau est au large de Douvres: the boat is off Douver.

Lent: à

> Meaning: slow
> Feminine form: lente
> Plural: lents, lentes

Tu es lent à réagir: you are slow to act.

Libre: à, de

> Meaning: free
> Feminine form: libre
> Plural: libres

Libre à toi de verifier si c'est bon: you are free to check if it is correct.
Il est libre de tout engagement: he is free from any commitment.
Je suis libre de faire ce que je veux: I am free to do what I want.

Lourd: à, de

> Meaning: heavy
> Feminine form: lourde
> Plural: lourds, lourdes

C'est lourd à porter: it is heavy to carry.
C'est lourd à digérer: it is heavy on the stomach.
La décision est lourde de conséquences: the decision is frought with consequences.
Il n'y a pas lourd dans le porte-monnaie: there is not much in the wallet.

Letter M

Malade: à, de

> Meaning: ill, sick
> Feminine form: malade
> Plural: malade

Elle est malade à en mourir: she is dreadfully ill.
Il est malade du coeur: he has heart trouble.
Elle est malade de jalousie: she is mad with jealousy.

Malheureux: à, de, en

> Meaning: unhappy
> Feminine form: malheureuse
> Plural: malheureux, malheureses

Il est malheureux de ne pas pouvoir te parler: he is upset at not being able to speak to you.
Il est malheureux au jeu: he is unlucky at gambling.
Il est malheureux en amour: he is unlucky in love.

Mauvais: en, de

> Meaning: bad
> Feminine form: mauvaise
> Plural: mauvais, mauvaises

Il est mauvais en français: he is bad at French.
Il ne serait pas mauvais de se renseigner: it would not be a bad idea if we got more information.

Médiocre: en

> Meaning: poor
> Feminine form: médiocre
> Plural: médiocre

Je suis médiocre en anglais: I am poor at English.

Moyen: en

> Meaning: average
> Feminine form: moyenne
> Plural: moyens, moyennes

Il est moyen en français: he is average at French.

Letter N

Natif: de

> Meaning: native
> Feminine form: native
> Plural: natifs, natives

Il est natif de Paris: he is native of Paris.

Nécessaire: à, de, pour

> Meaning: necessary
> Feminine form: nécessaire
> Plural: nécessaires

Les vitamines sont nécessaires à la vie: vitamins are necessary to life.
C'est nécessaire de le faire maintenant: it needs to be done now.
Ces outils sont nécessaires pour un bon travail: You need these tools to make a good job.

Nécessaire à + noun
Nécessaire de + verb
Nécessaire pour + verb or noun

Nouveau: à, en

> Meaning: new
> Feminine form: nouvelle
> Plural: nouveaux, nouvelles

Tu as du nouveau à ce sujet? have you anything new on this?
Il est nouveau en affaires: he is new to business.

Nul: en, de

> Meaning: nil, null
> Feminine form: nulle
> Plural: nuls, nulles

Il est vraiment nul en anglais; he is hopeless at English.
C'est bête d'avoir dit ça! It is stupid to tell that.

Letter O

Obligatoire: de

> Meaning: compulsory
> Feminine form: obligatoire
> Plural: obligatoires

Il est obligatoire d'aller à l'école: schooling is compulsory.
(however, L'école est obligatoire isthe most commun expression)

Originaire: de

> Meaning: originating
> Feminine form: originaire
> Plural: originaires

Il est originaire de Paris: he is originating from Paris.

Letter P

Pareil: à

> Meaning: likecompulsory
> Feminine form: pareille
> Plural: pareils, pareilles

Il est pareil à l'autre (il est pareil que l'autre): it is similar to the other one.
Il est pareil à lui-même: he does not change.
C'est du pareil au même: it comes to the same thing..

Perméable: à

> Meaning: permeable
> Feminine form: perméable
> Plural: perméables

C'est perméable à l'air? is it permeable to air?
Je ne suis pas perméable à ces idées: I am not receptive to such ideas

Plein: à, dans, de

> Meaning: full
> Feminine form: pleine
> Plural: pleins, pleines

Le sac est plein à craquer: the bag is full to bursting.
Il est plein aux as: he is very rich.
La maison est pleine de monde: the house is full of people.
Voilà une remarque pleine de sens: that's a very sensible remark.
Tu as mis plein de crème sur toi: You have got cream on you.
En plein dans l'oeil: right in the eye.

Possible: de

> Meaning: possible
> Feminine form: possible
> Plural: possibles

Il n'est pas possible de fumer: it is not possible to smoke.
Est-il possible d'annuler la réunion? Can we cancel the meeting?
Ce n'est pas possible d'être aussi bête: How can anyone be so stupid!

Près: de

> Meaning: close to, near

Je suis près de toi: I am near you.
La jupe est près du corps: this is a close-fitting skirt
Il est près de ses sous: he is tight-fisted
Il est près de minuit: it is close to midnight
Il est près de mourir: he is close to death
je ne suis pas près d'y retourner: I won't go back there in a hurry!

Prêt: à, pour

> Meaning: ready
> Feminine form: prête
> Plural: prêts, prêtes

L'appareil est prêt à fonctionner: the device is ready for use.
Le train est prêt au départ: the train is ready to leave.
Un repas prêt à emporter: a take-away meal.
Je suis prête à tout: I will stop at nothing.
Je suis prêt à partir: I am ready to go.
Tiens-toi prêt à venir: be ready to come.
Je suis prêt pour le départ: I am ready to leave.
Tout est prêt pour la réunion: everything is ready for the meeting.
(Je suis près de partir has the same pronunciation)

Proche: de

> Meaning: near, close to
> Feminine form: proche
> Plural: proches

Je crois qu'il est proche de la fin: I think he is close to the end.
Elles sont très proches de leur mère: they feel very close to their mother.
La boulangerie est très proche de la maison: the bakery is close to the house.

Profond: de

> Meaning: deep
> Feminine form: profonde
> Plural: profonds, profondes

Le puits est profond de 5 mètres; the well is 3 metres deep.

Letter R

Rapide: à

> Meaning: quick, fast, prompt
> Feminine form: rapide
> Plural: rapides

Il est super rapide à la course: he is a very fast runner.
C'est rapide à faire: it is quick to make, to do.
Il n'est pas rapide à la détente: he is not quick off the mark.

Rebelle: à

> Meaning: rebel
> Feminine form: rebelle
> Plural: rebelles

Il est rebelle à l'autorité: he is rebel against authority..

Réceptif: à

> Meaning: receptive
> Feminine form: réceptive
> Plural: réceptifs, réceptives

Il n'est pas très réceptif à la musique jazz: he is not very open to jazz music.
il n'est pas réceptif à tes conseils: he is not open to your advices.

Reconnaissant: à, de, envers

> Meaning: grateful
> Feminine form: reconnaissante
> Plural: reconnaisants, reconnaissantes

Il est reconnaissant à son père: he is grateful to his father.
Je suis reconnaissant de votre aide: I am grateful for your help.
Je suis reconnaissant envers vous: I am grateful to you.

Reconnaissant à or envers someone
Reconnaissant de something

Redevable: à, de, pour

> Meaning: indebted
> Feminine form: redevable
> Plural: redevables

Je suis redevable à Pierre: I am indebted to Pierre.
Je vous suis redevable de la vie: I owe you my life.

Redevable à someone
Redevable de something

Réfractaire: à

> Meaning: resistant, refractory
> Feminine form: réfractaire
> Plural: Réfractaires

Il est réfractaire à la discipline: he resists discipline.
La bactérie est réfractairee au traitement: the bacterium is resistant to the treatment.

Réservé: à

> Meaning: reserved, booked
> Feminine form: réservée
> Plural: réservés, réservée

J'ai une table réservée à mon nom: I reserved a table..

Riche: de, en

> Meaning: rich, full
> Feminine form: riche
> Plural: riches

Cette expérience est riche d'enseignements: this is a tremendous learning experience.
Le musée est riche de plusieurs milliers de tableaux: the museum is full of thousands of paintings.
Les gâteaux sont riches en vitamines: the cakes are rich in vitamins (high-vitamin cakes).
Une année riche en rebondissements: a year full of action.
Je ne suis pas riche en farine: I am not well-off for flour.

Letter S

Semblable: à

> Meaning: like, similar
> Feminine form: semblable
> Plural: semblables

Cette tasse est semblable à l'autre: this cup is like the other.

Seul: à, avec

> Meaning: only
> Feminine form: seule
> Plural: seuls, seules

Il est seul à pouvoir le faire: he is the only one who can do it.
Elle vit seule avec ses enfants: she is alone with her children

Simple: à, de

> Meaning: simple, easy
> Feminine form: simple
> Plural: simples

C'est simple à comprendre: it is easy to understand.
Il est simple d'esprit: he is simple-minded.
Nous nous verrons seul à seul: we will meet privately.

Sourd: à, de

> Meaning: deaf
> Feminine form: sourde
> Plural: sourds, sourdes

Il est resté sourd aux appels de son père: he remained deaf to his dad's appeals.
Je suis sourd d'une oreille: I am deaf in one ear.

Letter T

Tant: de

> Meaning: many, much

Il y a tant de pluie aujourd'hui: it is raining hard today.
Il a tant d'argent qu'il ne sait pas quoi acheter: he has so much money he does not know what to buy.

Triste: à, de

> Meaning: sad
> Feminine form: triste
> Plural: tristes

Je suis triste à l'idée que tu t'en ailles: I am sad at the idea you will leave.
Je suis triste de te voir partir: I am sad to see you go.

Trop: de

> Meaning: too many, too much

J'ai bu trop de jus de fruit: I drunk too many fruit juices.
Elle a trop de travail: she has got too much work.
Oh merci, c'est trop de bonté: oh thank you, it is too kind of you.
Il y a trop de monde: there are too many people.

Letter U

Unique: à, en

> Meaning: unique
> Feminine form: unique
> Plural: uniques

C'est unique au monde: it is unique.
Il est unique en son genre: he is one of a kind.

Utile: à, de

> Meaning: useful
> Feminine form: utile
> Plural: utiles

C'est utile à savoir: it is useful to know.
Je peux être utile à quelque chose? Can I help you with anything?
Ce n'est pas utile d'appeler tes parents: it is not necessary to call your parents.

C'est utile à for shorter sentences with nothing after the following word (verb or noun).
C'est utile de generally speaking or for longer sentences (verb).

Letter V

Vital: de, pour

> Meaning: vital
> Feminine form: vitale
> Plural: vitaux, vitales

Ce n'est pas vital de faire cela: it is not vital to do this.
L'eau est vitale pour l'homme: water is vital to humans.

Letter V

Letter A
absent
adhérent
adjacent
admissible
adroit
affamé
âgé
agile
agréable
allergique
amoureux
amusant
antérieur
applicable
appréciable
approprié
apte
attentif
avide

Letter B
beau
beaucoup
bienvenu
bon

Letter C
capable
capital
certain
complice
conscient
content
contraire
contrairement
correct
coupable
curieux

Letter D
davantage
dépendant
désireux
difficile
digne
distant
drôle
dupe
dur

Letter E
égal
enclin
épais
essentiel
exact
excessif
exempt

Letter F
facile
faible
fatigant
fidèle
fort
fou
friand

Letter G
généreux

Letter H
habile
heureux
honteux
horrible

Letter I
impardonnable
impatient
important
incapable
indifférent
injuste
inquiet
intéressant
inutile

Letter J
jaloux
juste

Letter L
large
lent
libre
lourd

Letter M
malade
malheureux
mauvais
médiocre
moyen

Letter N
natif
nécessaire
nouveau
nul

Letter O
obligatoire
originaire

Letter P
pareil
perméable
plein
possible
près
prêt
proche
profond

Letter R
rapide
rebelle
réceptif
reconnaissant
redevable
réfractaire
réservé
riche

Letter S
semblable
seul
simple
sourd

Letter T
tant
triste
trop

Letter U
unique
utile

Letter V
vital

Printed in Great Britain
by Amazon.co.uk, Ltd.,
Marston Gate.